LAKE CLASSICS

*Great Short Stories from
Around the World I*

WITHDRAWN

Alphonse
DAUDET

Stories retold by Prescott Hill
Illustrated by James Balkovek

LAKE EDUCATION
Belmont, California

LAKE CLASSICS

Great American Short Stories I

Washington Irving, Nathaniel Hawthorne, Mark Twain, Bret Harte, Edgar Allan Poe, Kate Chopin, Willa Cather, Sarah Orne Jewett, Sherwood Anderson, Charles W. Chesnutt

Great American Short Stories II

Herman Melville, Stephen Crane, Ambrose Bierce, Jack London, Edith Wharton, Charlotte Perkins Gilman, Frank R. Stockton, Hamlin Garland, O. Henry, Richard Harding Davis

Great British and Irish Short Stories I

Arthur Conan Doyle, Saki (H. H. Munro), Rudyard Kipling, Katherine Mansfield, Thomas Hardy, E. M. Forster, Robert Louis Stevenson, H. G. Wells, John Galsworthy, James Joyce

Great Short Stories from Around the World I

Guy de Maupassant, Anton Chekhov, Leo Tolstoy, Selma Lagerlöf, Alphonse Daudet, Mori Ogwai, Leopoldo Alas, Rabindranath Tagore, Fyodor Dostoevsky, Honoré de Balzac

Cover and Text Designer: Diann Abbott

Library of Congress Catalog Number: 94-075344
ISBN 1-56103-043-0
Printed in the United States of America
1 9 8 7 6 5 4 3 2

CONTENTS

Introduction 5

About the Author 7

The Last Lesson 9

The Old Folks 21

The Siege of Berlin 39

The Child Spy 57

Thinking About the Stories 77

❦ Lake Classic Short Stories ❧

"The universe is made of stories, not atoms."
—Muriel Rukeyser

"The story's about you."
—Horace

Everyone loves a good story. It is hard to think of a friendlier introduction to classic literature. For one thing, short stories are *short*—quick to get into and easy to finish. Of all the literary forms, the short story is the least intimidating and the most approachable.

Great literature is an important part of our human heritage. In the belief that this heritage belongs to everyone, *Lake Classic Short Stories* are adapted for today's readers. Lengthy sentences and paragraphs are shortened. Archaic words are replaced. Modern punctuation and spellings are used. Many of the longer stories are abridged. In all the stories,

5

painstaking care has been taken to preserve the author's unique voice.

Lake Classic Short Stories have something for everyone. The hundreds of stories in the collection cover a broad terrain of themes, story types, and styles. Literary merit was a deciding factor in story selection. But no story was included unless it was as enjoyable as it was instructive. And special priority was given to stories that shine light on the human condition.

Each book in the *Lake Classic Short Stories* is devoted to the work of a single author. Little-known stories of merit are included with famous old favorites. Taken as a whole, the collected authors and stories make up a rich and diverse sampler of the story-teller's art.

Lake Classic Short Stories guarantee a great reading experience. Readers who look for common interests, concerns, and experiences are sure to find them. Readers who bring their own gifts of perception and appreciation to the stories will be doubly rewarded.

❦ Alphonse Daudet ❧
(1840–1897)

About the Author

Alphonse Daudet was born at Nimes, France. His parents were small silk manufacturers of peasant background. The couple had 17 children, most of whom died young.

Schooled in Lyons, he wrote poetry and stories even as a boy. For lack of funds, he did not stay on at school to graduate.

But Daudet was ambitious. As a young man he went to Paris. There he quickly became even "more Parisian than the Parisians." He worked as a secretary to the Duc de Morny. This position gave him both security and prestige.

The handsome, curly-haired Daudet became a drawing-room favorite. He met the great writers and artists of his day and soon published his own work in popular magazines. At last, he was living the artistic life that he had always dreamed of.

The "great little novelist," as he was called, had the light touch. Like all of his French contemporaries, he was influenced by the great Flaubert. Yet his own sweetness and charm showed through in spite of himself.

Daudet's stories are sentimental, comic, and pathetic—a mixture of laughter and tears. He said that he tried to "show the mysterious beauty of life along with its crude truth."

Daudet wrote hundreds of stories and many novels. His complete works were published in 20 large volumes. A number of school texts have been made of his warm and humorous tales. It is said that he "probably has done more than any other to make French endurable to beginning students."

The Last Lesson

Is it human nature to take good things for granted? This thoughtful story is set in wartime. As the enemy approaches, something very valuable is about to be lost.

"FROM NOW ON ONLY GERMAN IS TO BE TAUGHT IN THE SCHOOLS OF ALSACE AND LORRAINE."

The Last Lesson

I was very late getting to school that morning and afraid that I would get a scolding. Mr. Hamel said that he would question us on spelling, and I hadn't learned my words.

For a moment I thought of running away and spending the day outdoors. It was so warm, so bright! The birds were singing in the woods. In the open field in back of the sawmill, the Prussian soldiers were drilling. It was all much more tempting than the spelling. But I did my duty and hurried off to school.

When I passed the town hall I saw there was a crowd in front of the bulletin board. For the last two years all our bad news had come from there. We read about the lost battles, the draft, the orders of the commanding officer. I didn't have time to stop, but I thought, "What can be the matter now?"

I hurried by as fast as I could go. I saw the blacksmith reading the bulletin. He called after me, "Don't go so fast! You'll get to your school in plenty of time!"

I thought he was making fun of me, and reached the schoolyard out of breath.

As school got started, we usually made a lot of noise. People could hear us out in the street. They could hear us opening and closing our desks. They could hear us reading our lessons out loud. And they could hear our teacher's big iron ruler rapping on the table.

But today it was all so still! I had counted on it being very busy. That way I might get to my desk without being seen. But, of course, that day had to be as quiet as Sunday morning. Through the window I saw my classmates, already in their places. Mr. Hamel walked up and down with his terrible iron ruler under his arm. I had to open the door and go in before everybody. You can imagine how frightened I was feeling.

But nothing happened. When Mr. Hamel saw me, he said very kindly, "Go to your place quickly, little Franz. We were beginning without you."

I jumped over the bench and sat down at my desk. I had gotten over a little of my fright. It was then I noticed that our teacher had on his beautiful green coat. He also wore his best white shirt, and his black silk cap. Usually he only dressed like that on prize days.

The whole school seemed strange and quiet. But something else surprised me even more. The benches in the back of the room had always been empty. But now a few of the village people were sitting there quietly. Old Mr. Hauser was there, and so were the former mayor and the former postmaster. There were several other people besides. All of them looked sad. Mr. Hauser had brought an old school book. He held it open on his knees with his eyeglasses lying across the pages.

While I was wondering about it all, Mr. Hamel walked to the front of the room. He spoke in the quiet and gentle tone that he had used with me. "My children," he said, "this is the last lesson I will be giving you. The order has come from the Prussians in Berlin.

"From now on, only German is to be taught in the schools of Alsace and Lorraine. The new teacher will be here tomorrow. This will be your last French lesson. I want you to be very attentive."

What a thunderclap these words were to me!

Oh, the wretches. So *that* was the notice on the bulletin board!

My last French lesson! How could it be? Why, I hardly knew how to write! I should never learn any more! I must stop there, then! Oh, how sorry I was for not learning my lessons. How sorry I was for the days I had skipped school. How could I have gone off looking for birds' eggs, or playing in the woods? Just a while ago my books had seemed such a bother. They'd seemed too heavy to carry. Now my spelling books and my history books seemed like old friends. I didn't want to give them up.

And what about Mr. Hamel? The idea that I should never see him again made me sad. It made me forget about how cranky he was.

Poor man! He had put on his best clothes in honor of our last lesson. Now I understood why the villagers were sitting in the back of the room. They were sorry, too, that they had not gone to school more. It was their way of thanking our master for his 40 years of faithful service. They were showing their respect for the country that was theirs no more.

While I was thinking of all this, I heard my name called. It was my turn to recite. I wanted to spell all the words without a mistake. But I got mixed up on the first word. I stood there, holding on to my desk, my heart beating fast. I didn't dare to look up.

I heard Mr. Hamel say to me, "I won't scold you, little Franz. You must feel bad enough. See how it is! Every day we have said to ourselves, 'Bah! I still have plenty of time. I'll learn it tomorrow.' And now you see where we've come out.

"Ah, that's the great trouble with Alsace," he went on. "We put off too much learning until tomorrow. Now those Prussian fellows out there will have the right to make fun of you. They will say, 'Ha! You pretend to be Frenchmen! Why is it you can neither speak nor write your own language?'"

Mr. Hamel smiled gently at me. "And you are not the worst, poor little Franz. We must all take the blame. Many parents in our town did not help their children learn. They put them to work on a farm or at the mills, to make money. And I? I've been to blame also."

Mr. Hamel shook his head sadly. "Have I not often sent you to water my flowers instead of learning your lessons? And when I myself wanted to go fishing—did I not just give all of you a holiday?"

Mr. Hamel went on to talk about the French language. He said it was the most beautiful language in the world. He said we must guard it among us and never forget it. When a people are made slaves, he said, they must hold onto their language. In the end, it will be like a key to their prison.

Then he opened a book and read us our lesson for the day. I was amazed to see how well I understood it. All he said seemed so easy, so easy! I think, too, that I had never listened so carefully. Never before had he explained a lesson with so much patience. Now it seemed that he wanted to give us everything he knew before he left.

Next he taught us a lesson in handwriting. On the blackboard Mr. Hamel had written in a beautiful round hand, *"France, Alsace, France, Alsace."*

"Copy those words," he said. You ought to have seen how everyone set to work—and how quiet it was! The only sound was the scratching of our pens on the paper.

Outside the window, the pigeons cooed very low. I wondered if the Prussians would make the birds sing their songs in German, too.

Whenever I looked up from my writing, I watched Mr. Hamel. He sat in his chair without moving, except for his eyes. First he looked at one thing, and then at another. I could tell that he wanted to fix in his mind just how everything looked in that little schoolroom. Just imagine! For 40 years he had been in the same place. He and his sister lived upstairs. Their garden was just outside the window.

In that long time, the desks and benches had been worn smooth. The walnut trees outside were taller. The vine that he had planted now curled about the roof. How it must have broken his heart to leave it all behind. Poor man! How sad it must have been for him to hear his sister moving about in the room above. She was packing their trunks! For both of them had been ordered to leave France early the next day.

But Mr. Hamel had the courage to hear every lesson to the very last. After the writing, we had a lesson in history. At the back of the room, old Mr. Hauser had put on his glasses. He shouted out the lesson along with us. You could see that he, too, was crying. His voice shook. It was so funny to hear him that we all wanted to laugh and cry at once. Ah, how well I remember it, that last lesson!

Then suddenly the church clock struck 12 noon. At that same moment, the trumpets of the Prussians sounded under our windows. Mr. Hamel stood up, very pale, in his chair. I never saw him look so tall.

"My friends," said he, "I—I—" But something choked him. His voice broke. He could not go on.

At last he turned to the blackboard and took a piece of chalk. Bearing down on it with all his might, he wrote as large as he could, *"Vive la France!"*

Then he stopped and leaned his head against the wall. In a moment, he made a gesture to us with his hand:

"School is dismissed—you may go."

The Old Folks

Have you ever been made to feel very, *very* welcome? In this charming story, a man visits his friend's grandparents. The reception he receives will warm your heart. Read on to make the acquaintance of a very memorable pair.

"Mamette, come here! This is Maurice's friend!"

The Old Folks

"A letter for me, Azan?"

"Yes, monsieur, and it comes from Paris."

My worthy old butler, Azan, seemed quite proud that it came from Paris. I wasn't. Something told me that this unexpected letter would make me lose my whole day. I wasn't mistaken—and you shall see why.

I opened the letter. "You must do me a service, my friend," it said. "Would you kindly close your mill for a day and go to Eyguieres? No doubt you know the

village. It is only about three or four
leagues from your mill—a pleasant walk.
When you get there, ask for the Orphans'
Convent. Go in without knocking—the
door is always open. As you enter, call
out in a loud voice. Say, 'Good day, worthy
people! I am a friend of Maurice!' Then
you will see two little old persons—oh!
but they are old, old, ever so old. They
will stretch out their hands to you from
their big armchairs. You are to kiss them
for me—with all your heart.

"Then you will talk. They will talk to
you of me, and nothing else. No doubt
they will say a lot of foolish things.
Please listen without laughing. You won't
laugh, will you? They are my grandparents—two beings whose very life I
am. They have not seen me in ten years.
Ten years—a long time!

"But how can I help it? The city of Paris
has such a hold on me! And they are too
old to visit me. If they tried to travel,
they would break to bits along the way.

Happily, you are *there*, my dear miller. In kissing you, these poor old people will fancy that they are kissing me. I have so often told them about you. I've talked so much of our good friendship that—"

"The devil take good friendship!" I said to myself. Why would it have to be *this* morning? Just when the weather is so beautiful! Why should I waste a day tramping along the roads? Today is too nice. There is too much warm southern breeze, too much sun. I wanted to stay home and enjoy it.

When that cursed letter came, I had just picked out a resting place. It was a grassy spot between two large rocks. I dreamed of staying there all day, like a lizard in the sun. My only plan was to drink in the light and listen to the song of the pines.

Well, I couldn't do that now. I shut up the mill, grumbling. I carefully hid the key. Then I got out my best walking stick, and off I went.

I reached the village of Eyguieres in about two hours. All of the streets were deserted. Everybody was in the fields. I heard the grasshoppers screaming from the elms in the courtyards. A donkey stood in the square in front of the mayor's office. He was sunning himself. A flock of gray pigeons splashed in the church fountain. But there was no one to show me the Orphans' Convent.

Then, happily, an old lady suddenly stepped out of her doorway. When I told her the place I was looking for, she directed me right to it.

Soon the Orphans' Convent rose up before me. It was a very large house, black and gloomy. Above its door was a stone cross with Latin words written around it. Next to the convent was another house, a very small one. It had gray shutters and a backyard garden. I knew this was the house I was looking for. I went over to it and walked in without knocking.

Even now I remember that long, quiet hall. The walls were rose-colored, and the air was cool. It seemed to me that I was entering a house from the olden days. At the end of the hallway, through a half-opened door, I heard the ticking of a clock. I also heard the voice of a child. The little girl was reading aloud. She read slowly: "Then—Saint—I-re-nae-us—cried—out—I—am—the—wheat—of—the—Lord—I—must—be—ground—by—the—teeth—of—these—an-i-mals."

I softly approached the door and looked into the room.

In the quiet half-light of a little room sat an old, old man with rosy cheeks. He was wrinkled to the tips of his fingers. I saw that he was asleep in his chair. His mouth was open, and his hands were on his knees. At his feet sat a little girl dressed in blue. She wore a cape and a linen cap—the orphan's uniform. It was this child's voice that I had heard. The book on her lap was bigger than she was.

She was reading about the life of Saint Irenaeus.

The girl's reading had a strange effect on the entire household. The old man slept in his chair. The flies slept on the ceiling, and even the canaries were sleeping in their cage. The great clock itself seemed to snore—tick-tock, tick-tock. Not a thing was awake or moving in the room but a broad band of light. That soft light shone straight and white through the cracks in the closed shutter.

Amid this general slumber, the child went gravely on with her reading.

"Then—two—li-ons—dart-ed—up-on—him—and—ate—him—up."

At this moment I entered the room. The lions of Saint Irenaeus, darting into the room, could not have made a greater show. A regular stage effect! The little one gave a cry. The big book fell, the flies and the canaries woke, the clock struck. The old man started up, quite frightened. I stopped short at the door and called out in a loud voice, "Good day, worthy people! I am Maurice's friend."

Oh, then! If you had only seen him, that old man! If you had only seen how he came to me with outstretched arms. He hugged me and squeezed my hands. Then he wandered about the room crying out, "Good heavens! Good heavens!"

All the wrinkles on his face were laughing. He grew red.

"Ah! monsieur—ah! monsieur," he said.

Then he went to the back of the room and called, "Mamette!"

A door opened, and I heard a sound like the trot of mice in the hall. But it was not mice, it was Mamette. What could be prettier than that little old woman? She wore a little cap and a brown gown. In the old-fashioned way, she carried a handkerchief.

The two old people were very like each other. If he had worn a gown and cap, he too might be called Mamette. But the real Mamette must have wept a great deal in her life—for she was even more wrinkled than he. Like him, she had an orphan with her. This little girl, in her short blue cape, never left the old woman's side. Clearly, these old people were being protected by those orphans. It was the most touching sight you could imagine.

On seeing me, Mamette started to make a deep curtsy. But a few words from the old man stopped her in the middle of it. "A friend of Maurice's," is all he said.

Instantly she began to shake. She wept and dropped her handkerchief. Her face grew very red, even redder than his. Those aged folk! They have hardly a drop of blood in their veins! Yet how it flies to their faces at the least emotion!

"Quick, quick! A chair!" cried the old lady to her little girl.

"Open the shutters," said the old man to the little girl next to him.

Then each one of them held one of my hands. They led me to the window to see me better. The armchairs were drawn up. I sat between the two on a stool. The little Blues were behind us. And then the questions began: "How is Maurice? What is he doing? Why doesn't he come? Is he happy?"

Yakety-yakety! and so on and so on for two hours.

I answered all their questions the best I could. I gave as many details about my friend as I knew. I made up others that I did not know. I was careful not to admit that I had never noticed many small things about his life. Did his window close? What color was his bedroom wallpaper?

"The paper in his bedroom? I believe it is blue, madam—light blue with lots of flowers."

"Really!" said the old lady, much affected. Then she turned to her husband and added, "He is such a dear lad!"

"Yes, yes, Maurice is a dear lad," said the other.

All the time I was speaking, they kept busy. To each other they gave little nods and laughs and winks and knowing looks. Sometimes the old man would lean closer to me and say in my ear, "Speak louder. She is a little hard of hearing."

And sometimes the request would come from her. "A little louder, please. He doesn't hear very well."

When I raised my voice, both of them thanked me with a smile. And by those faded smiles—as they bent toward me— I was quite moved. I could see in the old people's eyes a clear picture of their Maurice. My friend himself seemed to be smiling at me through a mist.

Suddenly the old man sat straight up in his chair. "Oh, I have just thought, Mamette—perhaps he has not had breakfast!"

Mamette threw up her arms. "No breakfast? Oh, heavens!"

I thought they were still talking of Maurice. I was about to say that the worthy lad had never in his life gone without breakfast.

But no, it was me they were talking about! When I said that I hadn't eaten, what a sight it was to see them hurrying about.

"Quick! Set the table, little Blues! Yes, that table in the middle of the room. Get the Sunday cloth and the flowered plates. And no laughing, if you please. Make haste! Make haste!"

And haste they made. After the little girls broke only three plates, breakfast was served.

"A very fine little breakfast," said Mamette, leading me to the table. "I'm sorry that you must eat it alone. We have eaten already."

Poor old people! At whatever hour you saw them, they would always say that they had "eaten already."

Mamette's good little breakfast was a cup of milk, a handful of dates, and a *barquette*—a kind of cake. It was just about enough to feed her canaries for a week. And to think that I alone ate up all that food! The little Blues whispered and nudged each other. And even the canaries in their cage—I knew what they were saying. "Oh! That awful, greedy man! He is eating up the whole *barquette*!"

I did eat it all, almost without noticing that I did so. I was so charmed by that bright little room. Everything in it seemed so sweet and old-fashioned.

I couldn't take my eyes off the two little beds. They were almost like cradles. I pictured the old couple in the early morning, still inside the fringed bed curtains. Three o'clock strikes. That is the hour when old people awaken.

"Are you asleep, Mamette?"

"No, my dear."

"Isn't Maurice a fine lad?"

"Yes, yes, a fine lad."

Just from looking at those beds, I could imagine their lives.

As I looked around, a drama was going on in front of the closet. The old people were very excited. They were talking about getting a jar of brandied cherries down from the top shelf. For the past ten years, they had been saving it for Maurice's return.

Now the old people wanted to open the jar for me. The old man was trying to reach up for the cherries himself. He climbed up onto a chair, to the terror of his wife.

Can you imagine the scene for yourself? The old man shaking on the tips of his toes. The little Blues clinging to his chair. Mamette standing behind him, breathless.

It was charming.

At last, after many efforts, they took the jar down from the closet. Along with it came an old silver cup. It had been Maurice's cup when he was little. This they filled with cherries to the brim— Maurice was always so fond of cherries!

And while the old man served them, he whispered in my ear, "You are very lucky to be the one to eat them. My wife put them up. Now you'll taste something very good."

Alas! His wife had forgotten to sweeten them! Those cherries were awful. My poor Mamette! But that did not stop me from eating them all without blinking.

The meal over, I rose to take leave of my hosts. Of course, they wanted me to stay longer and talk of dear Maurice. But the day was growing short, the mill was far, and I had to go.

The old man rose when I did.

"Mamette, bring me my coat," he said. "I will walk along with him as far as the square."

I felt very sure I knew what was in Mamette's heart. She thought it was too cool for the old man to be out. But she did not show it. She helped him put his arms into the sleeves of his coat. It was a handsome snuff-colored coat with mother-of-pearl buttons. Only then did I hear the dear creature say to him softly, "You won't be late, will you?"

He answered with a playful grin. "Hey! hey! I don't know. Perhaps not."

At that they looked at each other, laughing. The little Blues laughed to see the old folks laugh. In their cage, the canaries laughed too, after their fashion.

Daylight was fading as we left the house, the old fellow and I. A little Blue followed him at a distance. I saw that it was her job to bring him back. But he did not see her. He seemed quite proud to walk along, arm in arm with me, like any other man.

Mamette was beaming. I could see her watching us from the open door. The pretty little nods of her head seemed to say, "See there! My poor old man! But he can still walk about!"

The Siege of Berlin

Is it true that "what you don't know can't hurt you"? In this story a sick man's caretakers decide to protect him from disappointment. Amazingly, the old man feels stronger every time he hears a bit of war news.

THE OLD SOLDIER WOULD RETELL WAR STORIES FOR THE
HUNDREDTH TIME.

The Siege
of Berlin

As I walked down an avenue in Paris, I came to a big old building. Something made me stop and look up. All at once, my mind was flooded with old memories of the war between Prussia and France.

I'd visited an apartment in that building then. It was during the terrible days of August 1870. I was called there because I'm a doctor. Colonel Jouve, an old soldier, had suffered a stroke.

The old man had just rented that apartment at the beginning of the war.

Do you know why? Because it had a balcony overlooking the street. He wanted to stand there and watch our troops return in triumph! Poor old man!

The news of a terrible defeat had reached him at the breakfast table. He was shocked when he heard that the battle had been lost to the Prussians. It was then that the stroke hit him.

I found the old gentleman stretched out on the carpet of his bedroom. Standing, he would have seemed very tall. Lying down, he appeared to be immense. He had fine, noble features, beautiful teeth, and curly white hair. He was 80 years old, although he looked only about 60. Near him was his granddaughter, who looked very much like him. She was kneeling by the old man in tears.

The sweetness of the girl touched me deeply. She was the daughter and granddaughter of soldiers. Her father was on the staff of General MacMahon. Clearly, she was hit hard by the sight of this grand old man stretched out before her. It brought another terrible image to her mind. What if her father were killed in the war?

To the best of my ability, I comforted her about her grandfather. But deep down in my heart I was worried. At 80 years old, it is very hard to recover from a stroke.

For three days, in fact, my patient remained in a lifeless state. In the meantime, the bad news about another battle arrived in Paris.

Do you remember the strange way that news came to us? Until evening we believed it had been a great victory. It was said that more than twenty thousand Prussians had been killed. We even heard that the Prussian crown prince was taken prisoner. I do not know how old Colonel Jouve heard those first happy news reports. But he was clearly feeling the joy that everyone else in France was feeling.

That evening, I was very surprised when I came to his bedside. I no longer found the same man there. His eyes were almost clear, and his speech was much stronger. Now he had strength enough to smile broadly at me. Then he clearly said, "Vic-to-ry!"

"Oh, yes, Colonel Jouve. It *is* a great victory," I replied.

I gave him every detail I had heard about the wonderful success of General MacMahon. Then I saw his eyes relax and his face light up.

When I left the room, I found his granddaughter waiting for me. The poor girl looked very pale. She stood just outside the door, weeping.

"Why are you crying?" I said. "He is saved!" I took both her hands in mine.

The unhappy girl could scarcely find courage enough to answer me. The true report of the battle had just been given out. General MacMahon had not won the battle. The truth was that he was in flight and his entire army was scattered. We looked at each other in dismay. She was grieving at the thought of her father.

I was shaking at the thought of the old man. Certainly, he could not withstand this new shock. But what was to be done? Should we leave him his joy? It was his belief in our victory that had brought him back to life.

I told the girl that perhaps it would be necessary to lie.

"Yes, indeed, I will lie!" the brave girl said to me. Then she brushed aside her tears, and hurried back into her grandfather's room. There was a smile on her face.

It was a hard task that she had taken upon herself. But the old fellow's head was cloudy. He allowed himself to be fooled like a child.

When his health got better, the old

man's thoughts began to clear. We had to tell him of the daily movements of both armies. We drew up military bulletins for him. It was truly a pitiful sight to see that beautiful girl! Night and day she leaned over the map of Germany, sticking in tiny flags. She had to make up a whole glorious campaign.

Sometimes she would ask for my assistance, and I'd help her as best I could. But it was really the grandfather who helped us most in the imaginary invasion. After all, the colonel had fought against the Prussians years ago. France had won then. In his mind he had conquered Germany many times!

Colonel Jouve knew about all the strategies of war. "Now that's where they are going to go," he would say. "That's what they are going to do." He talked on and on.

In our make-believe game, his plans always worked out. That made him very proud. He had no idea that none of our news reports were true.

Day after day, we took cities and won battles. Yet we never went fast enough for him. Each time I arrived, I learned of a glorious new victory.

"Doctor, we have taken Mayence," the young girl would say. Then she would show me a sad smile.

Through the door I would hear a happy voice calling out to me. "They are on the march! In eight days we shall enter Berlin."

That was in his make-believe world. In the real world, the news was very sad. In truth, the Prussians were not more than eight days from Paris.

We asked ourselves if it would not be better to take him into the country. But how could we take him outside his apartment? Then he would be sure to learn the true state of France. He was still very sick. He was too weak from his great shock to be allowed to hear the truth. At last we decided to keep the old man in Paris.

On the first day of the blockade, I went upstairs feeling sad and upset. I was very worried. There is no feeling so terrible as when a battle is fought in your own city. But I found the old fellow cheerful and proud.

"Well," he said, "the siege has begun at last!"

I looked at the old man blankly. Had someone told him what was really happening? "Why, Colonel Jouve, how do you know?"

His granddaughter was sewing in the corner. She calmly turned toward me and said, "Oh, yes, doctor! It's great news. The siege of Berlin has begun!"

She continued to sew quietly. How could he doubt anything? He could not hear the cannons sounding in the distance. He had no chance to see how unhappy the people of Paris were. What

he *did* see from his window was a part
of the Arc-de-Triomphe. All about him in
his room were mementos of the First
Empire. In those years of his youth,
France was in its glory. His keepsakes
gave him the feeling that his beloved
country was still strong and free.

From that day on, our make-believe
war became easy indeed. Taking Berlin
was no more than a matter of patience.
From time to time, the old man became
bored. Then we would read him a letter
from his son. This would have to be an
imaginary letter, of course. There was no
news or any mail at all coming into Paris
anymore. All we knew was that the
French army had been suffering some
terrible losses.

Imagine the despair of that poor young
woman. How she must have suffered
without news of her father! Perhaps by
now he was a prisoner, being beaten or
starved. Perhaps he was sick. Still, she
had to make him sound strong and

confident in those happy make-believe letters.

Sometimes her strength failed her. Weeks would go by without news. At those times the poor old man became restless and could not sleep. Then suddenly, a make-believe letter would come from Germany. She would kneel beside her grandfather's bed and read to him in a happy voice. But all the time she would be trying to hold back her tears.

The old colonel would listen and smile knowingly. Sometimes he would explain to us what was going on. After all, he had once been a soldier! The letters he sent to his son were very noble and fine. "Never forget that you are a Frenchman," he would tell him. "Be generous to those poor people when you defeat them. Don't make them fear the invasion too much."

Along with these bits of advice, he would give his thoughts on politics. He had ideas about the terms of peace once we had defeated the Prussians. Upon that subject I believe that he was not unreasonable.

"Make them pay the cost of the war, and nothing more," he would say. "What good would it do to take their land from them? Is it possible to make France out of Germany?"

He spoke those words in a firm voice. I could feel the honesty in his words. He was a real patriot with a beautiful faith in his country. It was impossible not to be moved while listening to him.

During all this time, the siege continued. But it was not the siege of Berlin, sad to say. It was the siege of Paris! It was a time of intense cold, of heavy cannon fire, of sickness, and of hunger. But thanks to our efforts and tender care, the weak old colonel was not disturbed.

Right up to the end I was able to find a bit of fresh meat for him. There was only enough for him, of course. You could not imagine anything more touching than those meals of the old colonel's. The old man sat up in his bed, fresh and laughing. His napkin would be tucked under his chin. Near him sat his granddaughter. She was pale from worry and grief. But she guided his hands. She made him drink. She helped him to eat all those good things that were so hard to get.

Then, cheered by the tasty meal, the colonel would relax. He was safe in the comfort of his warm room. The cold winter wind was shut out. As the snow blew against the windows, the old soldier talked about his days in the army. He would retell old war stories for the hundredth time. He told of the army's awful retreat from Russia. Back then, he said that they had only frozen biscuits and horse meat to eat.

"Do you understand that, little girl?" the old colonel would say to his granddaughter. *"We ate horse meat!"*

I know how well she understood. For two months she had been eating nothing else. But as Colonel Jouve slowly got better from day to day, our job became much harder. Before, his senses had been dulled by sickness. That had helped us to keep up our game of make-believe. But now his senses were returning. Two or three times already the distant sound of explosions had made him jump.

We decided to tell him that the French had won a big battle near Berlin. We said that the cannons were being fired to celebrate the victory.

Another day, we had pushed his bed near the window. When he looked down, he could see our national guard troops. They were getting ready to defend against a Prussian attack.

"What are those troops doing there?" the old fellow asked. He shook his head and said between his teeth, "Bad discipline! Bad discipline!"

There was nothing to be done about it.

But we understood that from there on out we would have to be very careful. We couldn't let him know how bad things were for France.

Then late one evening the brave granddaughter came in to see me. She seemed very worried. "Tomorrow they are sure to enter the city," she said in a whisper.

Was the door of her grandfather's room open? I can't say for sure. But on thinking it over, I can recall something about that night. He had a strange look on his face. He probably did hear us.

Of course, *we* were speaking of the Prussians coming into Paris!

The old fellow was thinking that the French were *returning* to Paris. And he thought our troops would be coming home in victory!

It was the return for which he had been waiting so long. He had played it out in his mind many times. General MacMahon would come marching down the avenue. Flowers would be thrown into the air. Trumpets would sound. And his own son would be coming home.

Colonel Jouve himself would stand out on his balcony, saluting the French flag.

Poor old Colonel Jouve! He must have wondered why we didn't tell him about the victory. But then he must have reasoned it out. Of course! We wouldn't want him to get too excited.

He was careful not to speak to us about it. But the next day he went to the window. The Prussians had entered the city. They were starting to march down the avenue in front of his building!

The colonel stepped out onto the balcony. With great effort, he had dressed in his old army uniform. Now he stood there, very straight and tall. His great sword hung at his side.

He was surprised and shocked to find the avenue so empty. It was so silent! The shutters on all the windows were closed. Why was Paris so gloomy? There were flags everywhere—but they looked so strange. They were not the flags of France. And where were the people to greet our soldiers?

They were not there. Then from behind the Arc-de-Triomphe came the sound of music. But it was a German song!

A single voice pierced the air. It was an old, weak voice, but it was shouting out a fierce battle cry, "To arms!—To arms!—The Prussians are coming!"

As the Prussian army marched nearer, some of the soldiers looked up. Above them on the balcony they could see a tall old man. He stood still for a moment, and then fell to the avenue below.

This time Colonel Jouve was really dead.

The Child Spy

Have you ever done a thing that you then immediately regretted? In this touching story, a young French boy acts before he thinks. He earns a few coins for his deed. But the *real* price will be paid later—and by someone else.

"Let us pass, good sir. Our mother is ill and our papa is dead. My little brother and I want to look for some potatoes."

The Child Spy

His last name was Stenne, but everybody called him Little Stenne. He was a child of Paris, sickly and pale. He might have been 10 years old, or maybe 15. His mother was dead. His father was an old soldier who worked for the government.

Father Stenne took care of a square in Paris, keeping it clean. Everyone who came to the little park knew him. All the babies, the nurses, the poor mothers, and the old ladies in their deck chairs were his friends.

Everyone loved Father Stenne because of the way he treated them. And he took good care of the flower beds in the square. He kept the grounds neat and pleasant, and made sure it was a nice place to visit. Beneath his rough mustache was a good and tender smile. It was almost a motherly smile. To see it, people had only to say to the good man, "And how is your little boy?"

Father Stenne was happiest in the evening, after school-time. It was then that Little Stenne came for him. Then the two of them would go together around all the paths in the square. At each seat they would stop to greet the regular visitors and talk with them.

But everything was changed with the siege of Paris. Father Stenne's square was shut. Oil was stored there, and the poor man had been ordered to guard it carefully. Now he passed his life alone in the square. He couldn't even smoke his pipe because of the oil stored there.

He didn't get to see his boy until he got home in the late evening.

How angry he would get when he spoke of the Prussians! Little Stenne, for his part, did not find very much to complain of in the new life. A siege! It seemed so amusing to young monkeys like himself. No more school! No more homework! Holidays all the time and the street like a fairground.

Running about, the child stayed out of doors till evening. Sometimes he followed the soldiers of the national guard as they marched off to fight. His favorite regiments were those that had a good band.

And then there were the long lines! They started in the winter mornings at the butcher's and baker's. Along with everybody else, the boy would stand waiting, his basket on his arm. There friends met and talked about the war. As the son of Father Stenne, the boy was often asked for his opinion.

But the most fun he had was when he watched the *galoche* matches. Galoche was a game that the Breton soldiers played with a ball. They bet money on the outcome of the games.

Usually Little Stenne was either marching with the soldiers or hanging about the bakeries. Otherwise he was at the galoche matches. He did not take part, of course. He didn't have enough money. The boy was content just to watch the players. He admired one boy especially, a big fellow in a blue coat. When that boy ran, Little Stenne could hear coins clinking in his coat.

One day, the big fellow picked up a coin that had rolled toward Little Stenne. As he did, he said, "Don't you wish you had money? Well, if you like, I will tell you where to find some."

When the game was over, the big boy took Little Stenne aside. He told him how he could earn some money. All he had to do was to come with him to sell newspapers to the Prussians. At first Little Stenne refused. He was very upset with the big fellow. *The Prussians were the enemy! It was wrong to have any dealings with them!*

For three days, the shock of the boy's offer kept him from going back to the game. Three terrible days. Little Stenne no longer ate or slept. At night he saw piles of coins in his dreams. The shining coins rolled back and forth across the floor.

At last, the temptation was too strong. On the fourth day he went back to the galoche game. He saw the big fellow again. And he allowed himself to be talked into the plan.

The two boys set out early the next morning with their sacks on their shoulders. They had the newspapers hidden under their coats. It was just dawn when they reached the Flanders Gate. The big fellow took Little Stenne by the hand and walked up to the sentinel. He had a big red nose but a kind look on his face. The big boy said to the sentinel, "Let us pass, good sir. Our mother is ill, and papa is dead. My little brother and I are going to see if we can get some potatoes from the fields."

Then he broke into tears.

Little Stenne was full of shame. He bent his head to hide his feelings. The sentinel looked down at the boys for a moment. Then he glanced down the deserted, white road.

"Get along quickly," the sentinel said, letting them pass. And with that they were on the road to Aubervilliers. How the big fellow laughed!

As the boys walked along, they were not stopped. The big fellow knew the roads and stayed clear of the sentinels. But before very long, they ran into some French soldiers crouched at the bottom of a ditch. The big boy began to tell his story over again. But the soldiers would not let the two boys pass.

As the big fellow begged, an old sergeant showed up. He was pale and wrinkled. He reminded Little Stenne of his father. The sergeant said to the boy, "Now then, no more crying! You will be allowed to go look for potatoes. But first come in and warm yourselves a little. Your little brother looks frozen!"

Alas! It was not with cold that Little Stenne was shaking. It was with fear. It was with shame. In the guardhouse there were some soldiers squatting around a fire. It was a very small fire—just big enough to get the frost out of the soldiers' biscuits. They didn't have any cooking tools. They had to stick the biscuits on the points of their bayonets.

The soldiers pressed together to make room for the children. They gave them a little coffee to sip. While the boys were drinking, an officer came to the door. He called to the sergeant and whispered to him. Then he went off very fast.

"My boys!" said the sergeant, coming

back with a smile on his face. "There will be sport tonight. We have got hold of a Prussian password! I think that this time we are going to recapture Bourget." Little Stenne knew what this meant. Three bloody battles had been fought over this place. So far, the Prussians had always won.

There was an explosion of laughs and cheers. There was dancing and singing and polishing up of bayonets. Taking advantage of the uproar, the two children slipped away.

On the other side of the trench was an open field. Beyond the field was a long white wall. It had holes in it that the Prussian soldier could shoot through. Now the boys headed toward the wall. With every few steps they stopped, pretending to pick potatoes.

"Let's go back. Let's not go," Little Stenne kept saying.

The other boy only shrugged his shoulders and kept on his way. Then suddenly they heard the click of a rifle being cocked.

"Lie down," said the big boy, flinging himself on the ground.

Once down, he whistled. Over the snow, another whistle answered. The boys moved slowly ahead, crawling on all fours. In front of the long wall, just at ground level, they spotted a yellow mustache. The man who wore it also wore a dirty, flat cap. He was a Prussian soldier. The big boy jumped down into the trench beside him.

"This is my brother," he said, pointing to Little Stenne.

He was so little, this Stenne, that the Prussian laughed at the sight of him. He took hold of the small boy and lifted him up to the rim of the trench.

On the other side of the wall there were big banks of earth. Broken trees lay along the ground. Little Stenne could see black holes in the snow. And in every hole he saw the same filthy flat caps and the same yellow mustaches. The men who wore them laughed at the sight of the two children.

In a corner there was a gardener's house. The ground floor was full of Prussian soldiers. Some played cards. Others were making soup over a big fire. The cabbage and lard smelled good to the boys. How different from the camp of the French soldiers!

The officers were upstairs. The boys could hear them playing the piano and uncorking champagne bottles. When the boys went upstairs they were welcomed with a shout of joy. They handed over their newspapers. Then drinks were poured out for the boys, and they were made to talk.

All of these officers looked proud of themselves. The big boy amused them with his talk. He swore and used gutter slang. The Prussians laughed and repeated his words.

Little Stenne would have liked to talk,

too. He wanted to show that he was not a fool. But something stopped him. In front of him sat a Prussian who was older and more serious than the rest. He was reading—or rather, pretending to read. Actually, his eyes never left Little Stenne. There was tenderness in his face. Perhaps the man had a child of the same age at home. As he looked at Little Stenne, there was also sadness in his eyes. Perhaps he was saying to himself, "I would rather die than see my son follow such a trade."

From that moment on, Little Stenne felt as if a hand rested on his heart and kept it from beating.

He listened as the big boy made fun of the French soldiers. That got the Prussians laughing. Then the big fellow lowered his voice. The officers leaned forward and their faces became serious. Little Stenne couldn't believe it! The terrible boy was warning the Prussians! He was telling them about the coming attack by the French soldiers!

Little Stenne jumped to his feet. He was filled with anger. "Not that! You— you—I will not allow you. . . ."

But the big boy only laughed and went on. Before he had finished, all the officers were on their feet. One of them showed the children to the door.

"Out of the camp!" he said to them. Then the soldiers began to talk among themselves, very quickly, in German. The big boy walked out, proud as could be. He clinked his money in his pockets.

Little Stenne followed him, hanging his head. Then he passed the Prussian whose look had troubled him so much. He heard a sad voice saying, "Not pretty, that sort of thing. Not pretty at all."

Hot tears came rushing up in Little Stenne's eyes.

Once back in the field, the children began to run. Their sacks were full of potatoes that the Prussians had given them. They passed by the French soldiers' trenches without being stopped. They saw that the French soldiers were busy getting ready for the night's attack. Troops were silently gathering. The old sergeant was there. He was working hard to get his men ready for the fight. But he was doing his work with an air of happiness. When the children passed, he recognized them. Again he gave them a kind smile.

Oh, how that smile hurt Little Stenne! For a moment he thought of crying out. *"Don't go over there,"* he wanted to say. *"We have betrayed you."*

But his comrade had warned him. "If you speak, we shall be shot," he had said sternly. Fear kept Little Stenne from speaking out.

When they came near to Little Stenne's home, they divided up the money. Little Stenne listened to the sound of the coins clinking. The thought of having money to play galoche came to him. It made him change his mind about

what they had done. Now their crime
didn't seem like such a bad thing.

But when he was alone, how wretched
he felt! When the big boy finally left him,
Little Stenne's pocket began to grow very
heavy. The hand that had gripped his
heart now gripped it harder than ever.
Paris no longer seemed the same to him.

The people seemed to give him hard
looks—as if they knew where he had
come from. He heard the word *"spy"* in
the noise of the wheels of passing carts.
And he heard it even louder in the far-
off beating of the drums from the French
soldiers' camp.

At last he got home. He was quite
happy to see that his father had not yet
come in. He climbed quickly to his room.
He took the coins that weighed so heavily
on him and hid them under his pillow.

That night, Father Stenne was kinder
than ever. He seemed so happy when he
came home that evening. News of the
fighting had just come in. Things were

going better in the country. As he ate, the old soldier looked at his gun hanging on the wall. He said to his child, "Hey, boy, answer me this. How would *you* go for the Prussians if you were big?" Then he laughed his jolly laugh.

Little Stenne did not answer. He pretended that his mouth was too full to talk.

Towards eight o'clock there was the booming noise of cannons.

"It is Aubervilliers," said Father Stenne. "There is fighting at Bourget." The old soldier knew well where all the forts were.

Little Stenne's face grew pale. He pretended to be very tired, and went straight to bed. But he did not sleep. The cannons thundered again and again. Little Stenne knew that the French soldiers thought they were going to surprise the Prussians. Instead they would be ambushed themselves!

He remembered the kind French

sergeant who had smiled at him. Now he thought of that kind man stretched out on the snow. And so many others with him!

The price of all this blood was hidden there, under his pillow. And he was the son of Father Stenne—the son of a soldier!

Tears choked him. He heard his father walking in the next room and opening the window. Below in the square the call to arms sounded. The reserve soldiers were gathering there, getting ready to do battle. The wretched child could not keep himself from sobbing.

"What is the matter?" said Father Stenne, coming in.

The child could hold back no longer. He leaped from his bed and threw himself at his father's feet. At that movement, the shiny coins rolled to the floor.

"What is that?" said his father. "Have you stolen money?"

Then, all in one breath, Little Stenne told his father that he had gone among the Prussians. He told him everything that he and the big boy had done. As he talked, his heart began to feel free at last.

Father Stenne listened with a terrible expression on his face. When it was done, he hid his face in his hands and wept.

"Father! Father—" the child said.

But the old man gathered up the money. "This is all?" he asked.

Little Stenne made a sign that it was all. The old man took down his gun from the wall. He put the money in his pocket. Then he said, "Very well. I am going to give it back to them." And without adding a word, without even turning his head, he went out. Into the street he rushed to join the reserves who were going off to battle. He was never seen again.

Thinking About
the Stories

The Last Lesson

1. Many stories are meant to teach a lesson of some kind. Is the author trying to make a point in this story? What is it?

2. What period of time is covered in this story—an hour, a week, several years? What role, if any, does time play in the story?

3. Good writing always has an effect on the reader. How did you feel when you finished reading this story? Were you surprised, horrified, amused, sad, touched, or inspired? What elements in the story made you feel that way?

The Old Folks

1. All stories fit into one or more categories. Is this story serious or funny? Would you call it an adventure, a love story, or a mystery? Is it a character study? Or is it simply a picture the author has painted of a certain time and place? Explain your thinking.

2. Look back at the illustration that introduces this story. What character or characters are pictured? What is happening in the scene? What clues does the picture give you about the time and place of the story?

3. Who is the main character in this story? Who are one or two of the minorcharacters? Describe each of these characters in one or two sentences.

The Siege of Berlin

1. How important is the background of the story? Is weather a factor in the story? Is there a war going on or some other unusual circumstance? What influence does the background have on the characters' lives?

2. An author builds the plot around the conflict in a story. In this story, what forces or characters are struggling against each other? How is the conflict finally resolved?

3. Which character in this story do you most admire? Why? Which character do you like the least?

The Child Spy

1. Interesting story plots often have unexpected twists and turns. What surprises did you find in this story?

2. Is there a character in this story who makes you think of yourself or someone you know? What did the character say or do to make you think that?

3. Suppose this story had a completely different outcome. Can you think of another effective ending for this story?